nickelodeon™

SpongeBob SquarePants™

COMIC CRAZY...

Take 2!

SIMON AND SCHUSTER/NICKELODEON

Stephen Hillenburg

Based on the TV series *SpongeBob SquarePants*® created by Stephen Hillenburg
as seen on Nickelodeon®

SIMON AND SCHUSTER
First published in Great Britain in 2010 by Simon & Schuster UK Ltd
1st Floor, 222 Gray's Inn Road, London WC1X 8HB
A CBS Company

Originally published in the USA in 2010 by Simon Spotlight, an imprint of Simon & Schuster Children's Division, New York.

A CIP catalogue record for this book is available from the British Library

ISBN 978-1-84738-970-1

Printed in Singapore

3 5 7 9 10 8 6 4 2

"Turbo Snail," "Psychic Snail," and "Scary Noises": Story, art, and lettering by James Kochalka. "Accept No Substitutes!": Story by David Lewman; Pencils by Gregg Schigiel; Inks by Jeff Albrecht; Coloring by Sno Cone Studios; Lettering by Comicraft. "Fearless Cheeks": Story by Sam Henderson; Pencils and inks by Vince Deporter; Coloring by Stu Chaifetz. "Keep away from Krabs!": Story, art, and inks by Stephen DeStefano; Coloring by Sno Cone Studios; Lettering by Comicraft. "Krusty Karen": Story by David Lewman; Pencils by Gregg Schigiel; Inks by Jeff Albrecht; Coloring by Sno Cone Studios; Lettering by Comicraft. "Mermaid Man Cleans Up": Story by Derek Drymon; Pencils and inks by Ramona Fradon; Coloring by Matt Madden; Lettering by Ken Lopez. "The Big Race": Story, art, and lettering by Graham Annable; Coloring by Wes Dzioba. "Dance Contest": Story by Paul Tibbitt; Art and Lettering by Sherm Cohen; Coloring by Nick Jennings. "Staring Contest": Story and Art by Stephen Destefano; Coloring by Wes Dzioba; Lettering By Comicraft. "Fingers!": Story by Jay Lender; Pencils by Gregg Schigiel; Inks by Jeff Albrecht; Coloring by Sno Cone Studios; Lettering By Comicraft. "Drawings in a Bottle": Story and Layout by Derek Drymon; Pencils and Inks by Carl GreenBlatt (SpongeBob, et al.) and Ted Couldron (robot and Tree); Photo Panels by Nick Jennings; Lettering By Carl Greenblatt; Coloring By Digital Chameleon; Sprucey the Fighting Tree created by Anna S.; Tafu the Robot Created by Mat P. "SpongeBob Goes Casual": Story by Jay Lender; Pencils By Gregg Schigiel; Inks By Jeff Albrecht; Coloring By Sno Cone Studios; Lettering By Comicraft. "Hair Tonic": Story by Paul Tibbitt; Pencils and Inks by Erik Wiese; Coloring by Nick Jennings; Lettering by Sherm Cohen. "Hungry For Heroes": Story by Derek Drymon; Spongebob Art by Sherm Cohen; Mermaid Man Art by Ramona Fradon; Coloring by Sno Cone Studios; Mermaid Man Lettering by Rick Parker. "Molt Jolt": Story and Layouts by Jay Lender; Pencils by Gregg Schigiel; Inks by Jeff Albrecht. Coloring By Sno Cone Studios; Lettering by Comicraft. "Patrick's Pineapple Makeover": Story, art, and Lettering by Jay Lender; Coloring by Sno Cone Studios. "Sandy Goes on a Tear": Story by Sam Henderson; Pencils and Inks By Vince Deporter; Coloring By Stu Chaifetz; Edited by Dave Roman.

Special thanks to Stu Chaifetz. Nick Magazine SpongeBob comic staff: Andrew Brisman, Chris Duffy, Laura Galen, Tim Jones, Frank Pittarese, David Roman, Tina Strasberg, Catherine Tutrone, and Paul Tutrone. Nick Mag would like to thank Stephen Hillenburg, Derek Drymon, and Sherm Cohen.

TURBO SNAIL

ON YOUR mark...
get set...

...Go!

Whee?

PSYCHIC SNAIL

Can you guess
what I'm thinking,
Gary?

That's exactly
Right!
Nothing!

SCARY NOISES

What's that
SOUND?

CRUNCH

Oh! Ha ha.
It's just
Gary.

I was afRaid
it might be
Something scaRy!

ACCEPT NO SUBSTITUTES!

BE GOOD, GARY!

IT'S MY FAVORITE DAY--*BOATING SCHOOL DAY!*

SUBSTITUTE?!? BUT THERE *IS* NO SUBSTITUTE FOR MRS. PUFF!

SHE'S THE GREATEST TEACHER *EVER!*

MRS. PUFF IS SICK TODAY. PLEASE WAIT FOR THE SUBSTITUTE.

SK-REECH

EXCUSE ME, FELLOW STUDENTS...

...BUT I BELIEVE WE ARE SUPPOSED TO SIT QUIETLY WHILE WE WAIT FOR THE SUBSTITUTE TEACHER.

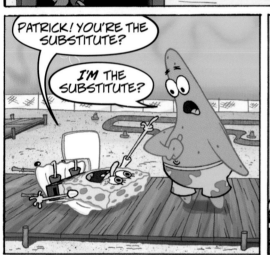

- 8 -

- 13 -

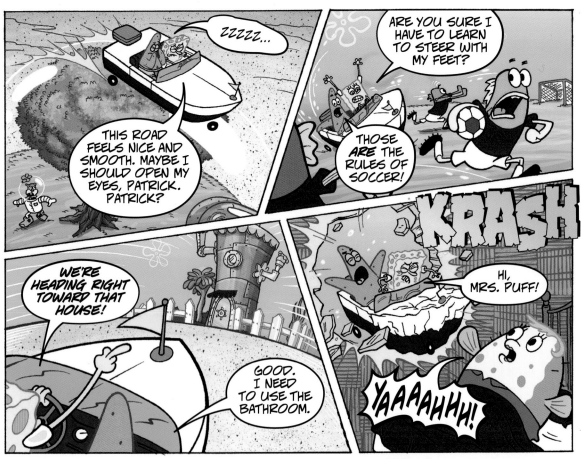

Fearless Cheeks

POW!

BOO!

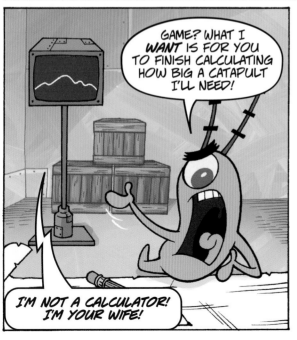

EAT AT THE CHUM BUCKET OR ELSE!

MY MOTHERBOARD **TOLD** ME NOT TO MARRY HIM!

≋SNIFF!≋

HMM...

GREETINGS!

SECURITY ALERT! SECURITY ALERT! THAT'S PLANKTON'S COMPUTER WIFE, MR. KRABS!!!

BRING YOUR OWN CUP DAY

NO, I'M MR. KRABS. HER NAME'S KAREN.

TO GET BACK AT PLANKTON, I'D LIKE TO HELP OUT AROUND HERE.

NO WAY.

I'LL WORK FOR FREE.

WELCOME ABOARD!

LATER...

WONDERFUL! LOOK AT ALL THAT MONEY! I MEAN, FOOD!

THIS ISN'T RIGHT! KRABBY PATTIES SHOULD BE MADE WITH *LOVE!*

BOYS, KAREN'S DOIN' EVERYTHING NOW, SO WHY DON'T YA TAKE A VACATION? WITHOUT PAY.

FOR HOW LONG?

DON'T CALL ME. I'LL CALL YOU.

SO, UH, KAREN... WHEN ARE YOU GOING BACK TO YOUR HUSBAND?

NEVER! UNLESS...

UNLESS WHAT?

UNLESS PLANKTON WINS ME BACK WITH ROMANCE!

AND SO...

OH, IT'S SPONGEBOB AND... THE OTHER GUY. HAVE YOU BROUGHT ME THE KRABBY PATTY SECRET FORMULA?

NO, WE'VE COME ABOUT YOUR WIFE.

WHERE IS SHE? YOU'VE GOT TO TELL ME!

SHE'S OVER AT THE KRUSTY KRAB.

THE BIG RACE

Just a little further...

Ahh...that's the stretch.

Hey, Squidward!

Yaah!

What are you doing?

I was in a deep stretch, SpongeBob! Don't sneak up on someone in a deep stretch!

I could've pulled something!

And that might have cost me the blue ribbon!

The blue ribbon?

Yes! For tomorrow's Bikini Bottom marathon!

I've been training for months for this run!

If I win, my picture will be in the paper! Everyone will know Squidward Tentacles in Bikini Bottom!

I'll be famous.

That sounds nifty, Squidward. Would you like a Coral Pop?

No!

My body is a finely tuned machine! I can't be putting junk into it!

The next day...

START

Welcome, folks! We're at the starting line for this year's Bikini Bottom marathon! Let's go meet some of the contestants, shall we? Exciting!

Hello there, sir. How are you feeling about this exciting race today?

Can't talk... conserving all energy.

312

Ha, ha! That's great! Just great! Let's move along here! Amazing!

312

I can't wait to do the real race!

I can't wait to eat a Coral Pop!

Hey, SpongeBob! I just saw Squidward's number on the ground!

Really?

Gosh, you're right, Patrick!

We've got to get this to him so he's ready for the real race!

When are we gonna have our Coral Pops?

There's the finish line!

Just got to push it a little further, then--

Hey, Squidward! Look what I have!

Yaaa!

We found your number on the--

GIVE ME THAT!

GIVE IT!

HA!

Hey, look!

SpongeBob won the warm-up race!

Amazing finish!

Later...

Hey, Squidward! You want a Coral Pop?

BIKINI BOTT

WINNER! SpongeBob

I didn't know I'd get a lifetime supply for winning!

Gaaah.

End

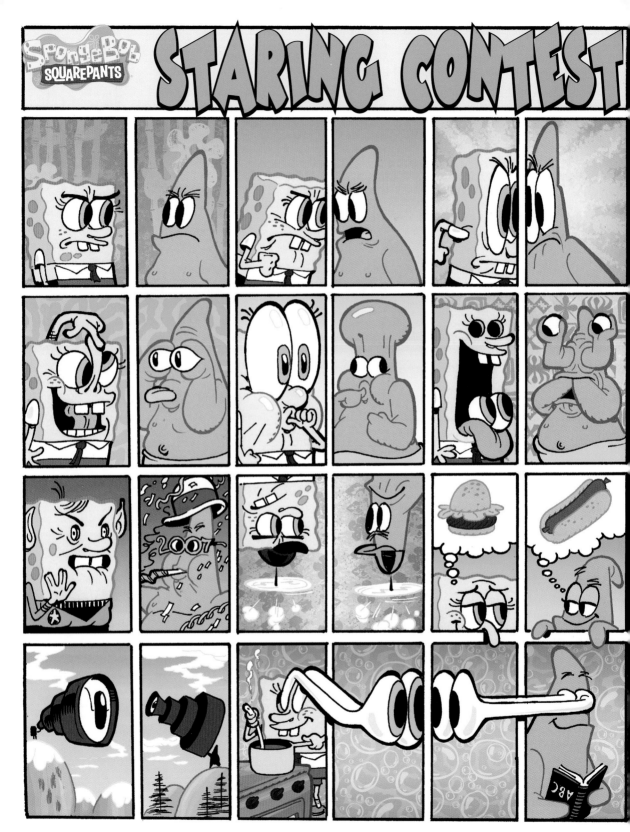

OH, NO!!

ALL OF THIS PRACTICE IN FRONT OF THE MIRROR HAS MADE ME LATE FOR MY STARING CONTEST!!

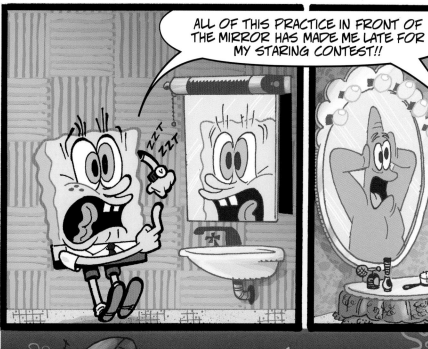

READY... SET...

...STARE!

FINGERS!

GO OUT FOR THE **BOMB**, SPONGEBOB!

I **GOT** IT, PATRICK!

WOO!

I AM THE **GRAB**-MASTER!

DIVE!

FAP!

SURE...THAT'S EASY WHEN YOU'VE GOT FINGERS.

HUH?

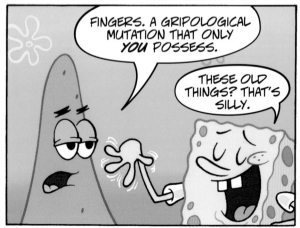

FINGERS. A GRIPOLOGICAL MUTATION THAT ONLY **YOU** POSSESS.

THESE OLD THINGS? THAT'S SILLY.

I'M NOT KIDDING, MAN, THESE THINGS ARE **WEIRD!**

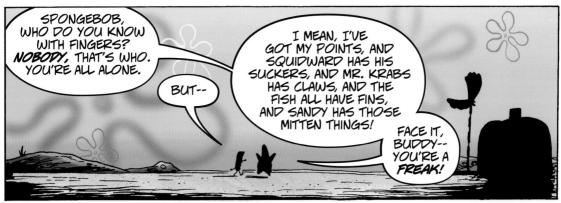

I KNOW YOU THINK *ALL* APPENDAGES ARE WEIRD, GARY...

...BUT FINGERS AREN'T *THAT* WEIRD, ARE THEY?

...

MEOW?

WHYYYYYYYYYYYY?

CURSE YOU, *FINGERS,* AND THE HANDS YOU RODE IN ON.

SO LONG, BIKINI BOTTOM...

YOU'LL NEVER SEE THESE DIGITS AGAIN.

BYE, GARY! I'M ALL DRESSED UP WITH SOMEWHERE TO GO!

BEEP! BEEP!

GOOD MORNING, MOTORIST! HAVE YOU *EVER* SEEN A UNIFORM THIS--

SPLASH

CLEAN?

PAAAATRIIIIIICK!

HI, SPONGEBOB!

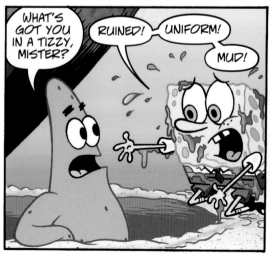

WHAT'S GOT YOU IN A TIZZY, MISTER?

RUINED!

UNIFORM!

MUD!

TRY *THESE* ON FOR SIZE!

I FOUND 'EM IN THE GARBAGE!

BIKINI BOTTOM BUGLE

FINEST DAILY NEWSPAPER

SPONGEBOB GOES CASUAL! BIKINI BOTTOM GOES WILD!

"I won't be needing THESE anymore!"

The SpongeBob Look!

BOUTIQUE OPENS

FREE BLEACH-BUTT JEANS WITH EVERY $1,000,000 PURCHASE!

"Just like SpongeBob wears!"

SPONGEBOB SIGNS WITH MODELING AGENCY

Move over, Tyra Bass, there's a new supermodel in town. Fierce fashion plate SpongeBob SquarePants has turned the runway into a FUNway with his outrageous, avant-garde styles. The hole-ier-than-wow Pants has just signed a contract with the elite Manta Management, and his salary is rumored to be in the bazillions. There's already buzz of a reality show, a movie deal, and an absorbing line of hair care products.

SPONGEB RECORD FIRST A

"THE WOR NEEDS M MUSIC!"

SpongeBob SquarePants

HAIR-TONIC

I'M BACK FROM WORK, GARY!

IT'S TIME FOR YOUR WALK.

MEOW!

GREAT HAIRDO!

OH, SO THIS IS YOUR SECRET.

MEOW?

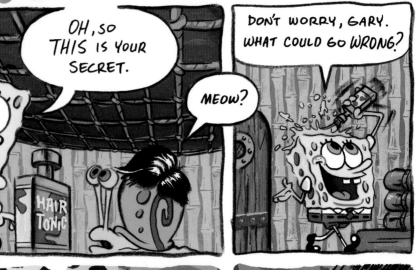

DON'T WORRY, GARY. WHAT COULD GO WRONG?

SpongeBob SquarePants

HUNGRY FOR HEROES

ARE YOU READY TO GO TO LUNCH, SPONGEBOB? I'M STARVING!

NO CAN DO, BUDDY!

I JUST GOT THE NEW ISSUE OF MERMAID MAN AND BARNACLE BOY COMICS AND I HAVE TO FIND OUT WHAT HAPPENS!

MERMAID MAN & Barnacle Boy

THE ADVENTURES OF MERMAID MAN AND BARNACLE BOY

RAAA!

HOLY SEA COW, MERMAID MAN! HOW CAN WE STOP IT?

LAST ISSUE, WE SAW A GIANT PIRANHA MONSTER ABOUT TO ATTACK THE DOMED CITY OF ATLANTIS!

ONE OF MY PATENTED WATER BALLS SHOULD GIVE HIM SOMETHING TO THINK ABOUT!

SPLISH

HUH?

SpongeBob SquarePants

Molt Jolt

THE KRUSTY KRAB

OH, *NO!* THIS IS THE WORST THING THAT'S EVER HAPPENED!

I'VE GOTTA TELL MR. KRABS!

MR. KRABS! I STOPPED TO MOISTEN THE PICKLE SLICES AND I *BURNED* THIS PATTY!

I'M *SO* SORRY!

MR. KRABS?

GASP!

BY BURNING THIS PATTY I'VE DESTROYED MR. KRABS'S *WILL TO LIVE!*

NEVER FEAR, GOOD SIR! I'LL RESTORE YOUR *JOIE DE VIVRE** OR DIE TRYING!

SOON...

WOOOOOOO!

A LITTLE ROLLER-COASTER ACTION WILL PUT YOU RIGHT BACK IN THE SADDLE, MR. KRABS!

*JOIE DE VIVRE MEANS "ENJOYMENT OF LIFE."

AND WHO DOESN'T ENJOY A GOOD BUDDY COMEDY?

RIGHT...BUDDY? HA-HA-HA-HA!

OR A SOOTHING *MONEY* BATH. I BET *THIS* GETS THE OLD JUICES FLOWING, HUH?

SEE?

YOU'LL FEEL BETTER WITH 40,000 VOLTS OF LIFE-GIVING ELECTRICITY RUNNING THROUGH YOU!

THANKS FOR THE EQUIPMENT, PLANKTON.

ANYTIME!

ZZAPP!

PAF!

SHRIEK!

WELL, I'M DONE!

SQUIDWA-A-A-A-ARD!

THE KRUSTY KRAB

SO WE WENT ON A ROLLER COASTER, AND THEN WE SAW A MOVIE, AND THEN HE *BLEW UP!!*

WHADJA DO? STICK HIM WITH THE *BILL?*

HEY, EVERYBODY! WHO'S FER *SOFT-SHELLED CRAB?!* AR! AR! AR!

MR. KRABS? AM I DREAMING?

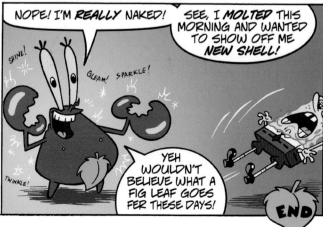

NOPE! I'M *REALLY* NAKED! SEE, I *MOLTED* THIS MORNING AND WANTED TO SHOW OFF ME *NEW SHELL!*

SHINE!

GLEAM! SPARKLE!

TWINKLE!

YEH WOULDN'T BELIEVE WHAT A FIG LEAF GOES FER THESE DAYS!

END